This Notebook Belongs To

....

Enjoying this Notebook?

Please leave a review because we would love to hear your feedback, opinions and advice to create better products and services for you! Also, we want to know how you creatively use your notebooks and journals.

Thanks for your support!
You are greatly appreciated!

Copyright © All Rights Reserved

Made in the USA
Coppell, TX
28 October 2019